BRANDING
You're Doing It Wrong!
A DIY Branding Workbook for Small Business Owners

Myishola Baker

Copyright © 2017 Myishola Baker

All rights reserved.

ISBN:978-1978394513
ISBN-10: 1978394519

DEDICATION

To My Andrew and Chika, Thanks for putting up with my Adult ADD, and more importantly thank you for fostering my creativity into something concrete.

To Jim, my SCORE mentor, Thank you for encouraging me to come out from behind the curtain and shine.

To my Parental Units, Thank you for never allowing me to be normal and perpetually forcing me to be the weird kid. It paid off!

Myishola Baker

BRANDING- You're Doing It Wrong!

CONTENTS

Acknowledgments   i

1   STOP IT!   1

2   Who do you think   13
    you're talking to?

3   Watch your tone   28

4   Don't let your   35
    cousin make your
    logo.

5   What's your   44
    catchphrase?

6   Those colors don't   49
    go together.

7   Social Media, Here   59
    we go!

Myishola Baker

ACKNOWLEDGMENTS

I would like to take the time to thank each, and every friend I have that has encouraged me, just called to say I was doing a good job, or who has referred a client. My friends are the ones who keep me moving in the right direction.

1 STOP IT!

Whether you know it or not, your business is being judged daily. Judged by how you chose to present it and its brand. From the colors chosen, to typography. Each and every piece makes a statement that tells consumers about you and your company. All it takes is one mistake to destroy your positive momentum, and if you're like most businesses attempting to brand in a digital world, you're doing it wrong.

Too many people overlook branding as something that's "not for them, doesn't matter to their business, or isn't something that will make a difference to the bottom line. Majority of businesses don't benefit from branding as much as they could or should for that matter, simply because they are thinking of it entirely wrong. You're probably thinking of branding as a name or a logo, maybe something to do with marketing. It's all rainbows and pretty things that have nothing to do with your actual business and is completely ornamental.

You Are Wrong.

Branding is your biggest and best asset. If done right, its only appreciates, and NEVER depreciates.

Go ahead and try to think of another company asset that is capable of that! Only a brand can. For example, would you rather have 10 bricks-and-mortar hospitals, or own the brand of St Jude? Would you rather have 20 bottling and packaging companies or the Budweiser Brand? 50 fast food restaurants ... or own the Mc Donald's Brand. You can put a Mc on anything and people will buy it. McBook? Good as sold!

In my 10 years in the branding industry, I will tell you that the most logical way to think about a brand – is as your child. Your company brand is just like a child. You chose how it looks, how it speaks and even who it associates with. The more you do this, the more it becomes a memorable and expected thing. Think of your friend that has a very distinct look. You can most likely go to a store and see and outfit and think to yourself, Martha would wear something like that. Another example is set behavior. If you have a child, and someone gives you a report about their behavior, your child has a distinct personality that would lead you to be able to decide whether it is something your child would do. Your brand encompasses both of those characteristic sets. Someone should be able to see an image you post, or an article you publish and know it was from your company without ever even seeing your logo. Your brand should be so strong consumers can identify it because it is consistent and predictable across the board.

Building a memorable brand takes extensive work, time and coordination. That being said, it only takes a moment to lose everything you've worked hard for. Take a note from the book of Enron. That brand is done for. No matter what they come out with next, more than likely you will not be interested.

The moment you understand and equate "Brand" to who your company is as a person, you will in turn grow more and more protective of it. You will guard it like it is your only child, policing those who speak for it. Branding is everything! It is your companies voice, appearance, style and face. It is what other companies see in your interactions and what your consumers see during each impression. Just as you would not want to go outside with wrinkled clothing, do not let your company go out with a wrinkled brand.

While thinking about your brand as a person, you should consider measuring the effectiveness of your brand. This is the report card of your "child". Measuring performance and reception is the only way to know if what you are doing is working to your benefit.

Pair measurement of your brands performance with treatment as a child and you are then in the prime position to craft your biggest asset. It is up to you, the leader of your company to take control and own your brand. You are already aware of this, as have many other small business owners. I am going to take a wild guess and say that you have been attempting to manage your brand on your own. Before we can build a great brand, it is important to take a moment to ensure you are not making any of the common mistakes owners have no clue they are making. Don't worry no one will know but you. As we go through our "Don'ts" mentally make a checklist of what you may need to correct.

1. Going With Your Gut

Everyone loves their business idea, otherwise they would not dedicate the time and energy it takes to grow it. Unfortunately, just because you think it is a great idea does not automatically make it so. The rest of the world may have absolutely no need for an underwater basket weaver. No matter how much you love it, it may just be a hobby. If there is no demand for your product or service, no amount of branding will save the business from its demise.

Instead, make time to ask others their interest in your product. Get real feedback from friends as well as strangers. It is important that your business meets a need, and does so in a way that is unique to you. Going with your gut on the answers to these questions is a surefire way to fail hard and fast.

Essentially, by going with your gut you're essentially flying blind and have no way of even knowing if a single soul wants what you have to offer until it's too late. Your brand may not be the issue at all, it could be your company.

2. Not Asking What The Consumer Likes

Piggybacking off number 1, number two is a similar problem. Odds are, if you are not asking for feedback about your company, you are not asking for feedback as to what interests your target market. It is extremely important to ask those in your target market what are their priorities. What means the most to them as they are choosing a company to meet their need? What are their deal breakers? What makes them come back?

The most effective brands speak specifically to the wants and needs of the target market. It needs to assure them, they can get their needs met in the way they prefer, with your company. This is the only message your brand needs to resound, and it needs to do it in every single facet.

Many owners decide the message of the brand sole based on what they would like to highlight or what they think is the best thing about their business. This is the wrong approach. Surveying and gathering data before you begin to build your brand is the tried and true method to ensuring your hard work is effective.

3. Not Being Consistent

When you've been sticking with the same branding elements for some time, it can be tempting to want to change somethings up to add a little excitement to what you may see as a mundane brand. This is wrong. Think of your "child" like a cartoon character. What would Doug be if they didn't have him wear a white shirt and green shorts? Would you even know Gretchen from Recess if they took away her glasses and ponytails?

I'm not saying you should never ever change your brand image. Your brand will evolve as time progresses. What is important however, is that it is planned, thought-out and has a purpose. There should be no random decisions to make your logo red if your brand colors are blue and white.

Even subtle differences can cause distrust in your brand. A slight deviation from colors or a different font that usual. Consistency allows your audience to know what to expect from you and rely on that expectation. Once you work to build a solid stable brand, why disrupt it because of boredom?

Taking time to be consistent and deliberate in your messaging will overall produce a brand that works for you instead of against you.

4. You Are Failing At Social Media

As I've stated, a strong brand is just like your child. It is unique with a specific look, feel and even voice.

Majority of small business owners fail to find that voice for their brand.

Think about exactly who you are as a company, what are you good at, what makes you a better decision that your competition? If you have those answers, you can create a voice and persona that will broadcast those messages across your social media platforms.

Unlike an Instagram models page, this must be genuine. Do not waste time trying to be like another page, or even trying to appear grander than you actually are. If you spend time putting forward the image you want other to perceive as you, your audience will be able to tell. Use who you are to your advantage by highlighting your strengths and playing up what makes you shine brighter than the other guy. Your audience will that you for it with their loyalty and trust.

5. Putting Yourself In A Box

Marketing yourself is like selling yourself in an interview. Your beliefs about your capabilities and worth will shine through whether good or bad, even if you attempt to mask them with confidence.

Namely, your thoughts and beliefs about what you deserve, how much you can grow and how great your product and service is. If you do not actually believe in your company and the things you say about it, it will be nearly impossible to convince others to buy in.

Never let self-doubt hold you back in any way. You ARE good enough. You DO deserve to be a large company. You CAN handle it. You are greater than you have ever imagined. The possibilities for you are endless.

If negative talk is holding you back, I suggest you get some affirmations and fast! The really do work.

Exercise 1
Gather Consumer Feedback

Find at least ten friends and family that have interacted with your business as well as 10 customers and proceed to ask them the following questions.

How they would feel if your product or service no longer existed anywhere?

_____
_____
_____
_____

What would they use instead if they could no longer get your product or service?

_____
_____
_____
_____

Why do they choose to work with your company to meet their needs?

_____
_____
_____
_____

Is there anything you can do to improve?

_____
_____
_____
_____

Once you have this information, find the commonalities among them. This will help you narrow the scope as to what is important to your target market. Later we will use it to tailor your messaging in a way that is memorable, and compelling.

2 WHO DO YOU THINK YOU'RE TALKING TO?

As I have previously stated, the cornerstone of any brand is understanding who your target audience is. Your company is not for everyone. Everyone is not your customer, and you don't want them to be.

Often business owners are too caught up trying to be everything to everyone to gain them as customers. Instead they should be focusing on becoming the ultimate solution to one specific targeted audiences need.

As we go through this journey of building a brand, we will need to hand select who will get the privilege of being the sole subject of our attention.

It is not enough to say "women" or "teachers", the more specific the better. You may want to it narrow down to where they work, what they eat, and how much they earn.

To better illustrate, here are a few suggestions:

- Single moms between the age of 22-30 who run
- Internet addicted gamers who live with parents
- College graduates who are unemployed in Texas
- Professionals who are too busy to grocery shop

The trick is to define the ideal person for your business and look to create messaging that speaks directly to their needs. If you own a pizza place with a jungle gym in the suburbs, you may want to target stay at home moms who have children between the ages of 4-10. You will want to look at what they like to do, where they congregate, what type of pizza they like to feed their children. Study your target, learn everything there is to know about them. Use what you know about your target to reel them in.

Being a small business owner, you cannot afford to target

everyone. Marketing costs money, as does research. The more targets you have, the more expenses will accumulate and worse, the accuracy of hitting your target goes down. It just does not make sense to do so. Two targets max. Anything outside of that will be a bonus.

Limiting your targets to two does not mean we exclude everyone else on the planet. Take money from whoever would like to legally give it. What it means is focus your dollars and energy on the people who are more likely to be your customer and ultimately give you money. This approach is much more effective, and easier on the budget.

An example would be an amusement park. Sure, everyone can enjoy something at an amusement park. The park's best route would be to look for a market of people, not too old, preferably with children who are old enough to ride and a disposable income. This group is most likely to purchase tickets to the park. Do we not care about college students? Of course, we do! However, we will focus our marketing on the families with children and disposable income. The amount of college students with extra money is dismal, and they likely have outgrown the initial excitement for amusement parks. They are not as likely to spend money at the park therefore they are not the ideal target market.

On the other hand, a neighborhood bar that offers air hockey and free pizza with a drink may find a gold mine in college students. The bar is in a prime position with this market because they cater to the priorities of many students. (Free food, Games and Alcohol). However merely stating the target market is college students is not enough. Not all students are of legal drinking age. Males are more likely to gravitate towards competitive bar games. It would be wise to further narrow the scope to male college students who are upperclassmen. Because we have chosen a specific target, we are able to research where to find them, where they like to spend their time and how they like to receive information. We then use that information when making decisions on building our brand to attract them.

Now that you have a good understanding on the why and the how, it is time to define your market.

Exercise 2

Define your Target Market

1. Take a look at who your customers are

Who are your current customers, and why do they buy from you?

_____
_____
_____
_____

Look for any commonalities. Who are the customers that bring in the most orders? Chances are if you had 100 more of those customers you would be better for it.

_____
_____

_____
_____

2. Pay attention to your competition

What's going on the other side of the fence? What seems to be your competitions target market?

_____
_____
_____
_____

Who do they have as customers? This isn't to compete with them or steal their customers. This is to take the opportunity to find a niche they may be overlooking and capitalize on it.

_____
_____
_____
_____

Write out a list of each special thing about your product or service. Next to each thing, list the benefit to having it (and the benefits of those benefits). For example, think of a chef. His feature is delicious healthy food. The benefit is a satisfying, nourishing meal. This can bring in more customers because they will want to try the food.

_____
_____
_____
_____
_____
_____
_____
_____
_____
_____
_____
_____
_____

Once you have your benefits listed, make a list of the specific type of people who have needs that can be met by your benefit.

_____
_____
_____
_____

This may still be a bit broad, and so we now move to number 3.

3. Narrow your base by demographic

It is important in this step to not only look at who may benefit from your product, but also who is most likely to spend money with you. A few factors to consider include.

Location:_____

Gender:_____

Income level:_____

Education level:_____

Marital or family status:_____

Occupation:_____

Ethnic background:_____

4. Be sure to consider psychographics

This means include characteristics that are more personal to the individual target base. These include:

Personality

Values

Interests/hobbies

Lifestyles

Behavior

Begin by writing down how your company fits into your targets life.

_____
_____
_____
_____

How exactly do they interact with your company?

_____
_____
_____
_____

Which features are most beneficial to them?

_____
_____
_____
_____

Where do they get their information?

_____
_____
_____
_____

Do they use word of mouth referrals from friends or family?

_____
_____
_____
_____

Do they pay attention to ads in magazines?

_____
_____
_____
_____

Do they even read magazines at all?

_____
_____
_____
_____

What about the newspaper, online searches, or events?

_____
_____
_____

Which section has the income to spend on your company?

_____
_____
_____
_____

If your product or service is affordable, is it seen as a budget item?

_____
_____
_____
_____

Will your target be open to purchasing with this perception, or do they value luxury?

_____
_____
_____
_____

4. Evaluate Your Decision

Once you've decided on a target market, answer these questions to evaluate whether you have created a market that will be receptive and beneficial to your business.

Will the target you chose find your product or service necessary?

_____
_____
_____
_____

Do you fully understand what moves your target to make purchasing decisions?

_____
_____
_____
_____

Can your target market afford your product/service?

_____
_____
_____
_____

Are they easily accessible? Can they be identified relatively easy?

_____
_____
_____
_____

Be sure not to break down your market too far. If you start researching and find there are only a few people who fit all your criteria, then perhaps you may need to look into a new market. It's a balancing act but it can be done. The trick is to make the niche small enough to cater to, but large enough to have a continual stream of income.

If you are having trouble gathering this information, that is ok. There are entire departments at larger companies who spent their full workday gathering information. It can be a daunting task, but there are some tools to help you started.

Fact Finder is an invaluable tool powered by the census. You can search and gather information by occupation, topic, race or origin, household income, family size and even limit it to your specific city or state. This is great for assessing the size of your target market and your access to them.

Learning about the habits of your market can be as easy as an online search. Chances are there are already blogs and articles written about your industry and the habits of those who frequent it. Take the time to read as much as possible so that you can gather a consensus among your research. Use it to evaluate and decide as to whether or not you would like to pursue your chosen market.

If you have successfully completed the exercise, you should have a well-defined market. Now you will be able to save lots of time and money, as well as be more effective. Long gone are the days of aimlessly targeting everyone who meets your branding efforts. Congrats!

3 WATCH YOUR TONE

"Voice" and "Tone" are for more than words they teach you in marketing class. In short, your brand voice is the essence of the persona. Remember our child? It has a voice, and that voice can attract or repel. Are they sweet? Sassy? Do they have the personality of an old friend you've known for years? Well, it all depends on the goal.

Get it? No? Let me explain further.

Pretend you are going to an event in which you do not know one person. This is a very important event and everyone there is a potential customer. You would like to leave the event with those potential customers having a good opinion of you. Because of this you chose what to display depending on your market. You may not tell certain jokes that may offend them. Perhaps you use a witty comeback that is playful and warm. Before you left the house, you picked your clothing carefully. Each decision speaks for you and your personality. From the shoe laces you chose to the haircut, they all say something. That is your voice.

It is the exactly same way with brands. Your company is the person going to the event. The bones of brand voice winds down to personality—setting many traits, specifically chosen for their attractiveness to your target market, in order to create an identity. Then, communicating the identity in a way that highlights those chosen traits. Pretty much, your brand must become its own person, built by you.

So what type of person should your child be? How do you choose the traits?

Your brands personality traits should be based on your target markets preference. A boutique for little girls will not have the same voice as a tailor for business professionals. Each decision about the brand, from the type of font, to the colors used, all the way down to where it is seen, should be strategic to the preferences of those you are trying to reach.

For example, take the dress boutique for little girls. Your target would likely be mothers of little girls and the little girls themselves who will go and ask their mothers to take them to your boutique. You may want to choose colors that evoke happiness and attract little girls. Blue would not be a very good color choice, even if it is your favorite color. You will want to use a font that is thin and dainty, or maybe a type of script versus a thick bold heave font. Even the smell when you walk in the store would be intentional. The smell of aftershave would not be consistent with the brand at all. The smell of cupcakes on the other hand, would be a good idea. It is important to make decisions that will reel in your target market and make them feel that your company was created with their needs in mind.

Furthermore, just as your mother's voice in your head comes up, and you know exactly what she would say when you're doing something wrong, your brand's voice should also be so consistent that others know what to expect. To remain consistent, you must first define your voice.

The following exercise will walk you through the process of designing the perfect persona.

Exercise 3

Finding Your Brand Voice

Every single one of your decisions will say something to consumers. Your brand should speak clearly and be concise. Use this exercise to define your brand voice.

1. Personify

Is your child male or female?

_____

Are they young or old?

_____

Are they serious, or funny?

_____

Are they loud, or subtle?

Do they comfort, support or encourage?

_____

2.Brainstorm adjectives.

Think of three or four adjectives to describe your child. Remember to assign characteristics that your target market values.

_____
_____
_____
_____

3.Go to the market.

Go research online. Check Twitter, Facebook, online forums, Pinterest even. Study how your target market communicates with each other. Learn their lingo. Is there a particular way they address each other? Write your observations.

_____
_____
_____
_____
_____
_____

4. Pick an ambassador in your head.

A way to really drive home your brand identity is to choose a celebrity you would pay to be an ambassador to your brand. It can be anyone dead or alive. Assume money is no problem and you have the budget to pick the best. Now think about what made you pick them.

What characteristics did your celebrity have that your market would find attractive?

_____
_____
_____
_____

5.Put it all together.

Once you've written down all the characteristics and attributes, find the ones that appear multiple times. These are likely good contenders. Make a comprehensive list and read it to others. Ask their opinion on it in relation to your brand. Does it make sense? Does it convey messaging that your market will be receptive to?

_____
_____
_____
_____

4 DON'T LET YOUR COUSIN MAKE YOUR LOGO

Your logo is important. I cannot stress this enough. It is the face of your brand. If you have a cheap or weak logo, the perception of your company's worth is dramatically lowered. The right quality logo can make your company appear well established just as easily as the wrong one can have others perceive you as an amateur or hobbyist.

Logo design is a lot more complicated than you might think. Sure, anyone can technically create a logo, just as anyone can cook, but it doesn't mean it's any good.

You may really like your logo; many business owners do. That is A OK! However, we all have those photos from high school that are extremely embarrassing to us now. Think back, you loved your hair and clothes on the day you took that picture. As my mother would say, when you know better, you do better.

And a lot of us need to do better.

A logo is art, and there is no "wrong" way to create art. You can even argue that logos cannot be "wrong" because they are the expression of the owner. You would be correct. However, your logo could be emitting the wrong expression. You may believe your logo says competent when in reality it says clueless.

There are some huge no-no's that I see daily working with small business owners. This section is dedicated to ensuring you know that they are, so that you do not do them. If you are already committing these sins, stop. I promise it's not doing you any favors.

1.) Using Clipart

Clip art is not a logo! Clip art is not a logo! Clip art is not a logo!

There I have said it! This includes photos you have pieced together from Google, images you cut from, all of it! It is not a logo!

Can you tell how passionate I am about this?

When people see your clip are logo, they immediately thing to themselves that you are new, lazy, cheap and have no idea what you are doing. Even worse, clip art is not custom for you. This means that others are likely to use it for their mishap-pen, poorly thought out logos. Now, your logo is not only disappointing, it's not even original. Because you used clip art I would put 100 dollars on a bet that it is not a png file and has a white background behind it. which takes me to number 2.

2. Not having the proper format

It is imperative that your logo be available in multiple formats for it to serve a number of purposes. There is no catch all format for your logo. If your logo is in only one format (probably jpg) you're doing it wrong.

While there are many needed formats, the most important

to know are the following two.

A png as I mentioned before will take care of that white background stopping you (hopefully) from putting your logo on anything other than a white piece of paper so that you don't see an unsightly white square. png files are made to be transparent. It allows you to add it to letters, brochures and other items without the background. It does not however allow you to send it as a standalone. Because there is no background, it will be difficult to read if sent on its own.

Vector is a format that mathematically draws your logo so that no matter how big or small you make it, there will be no distortion. If you have ever tried to make a small jpg image fill and entire page, you understand why you need a Vector image. This should be the format you send for your print work, signs, and other large items. You do not want a pixelated sign, or a blurry shirt.

3. Not making the logo scalable

This is another one that grinds my gears. Your logo may look great with the scriptures going around it, and the extra detail in the leaves in the trees while it is 4 inches tall. What happened when you scale that doing to an inch? Or half an inch? Can you still tell what it is? Or does it look like a jumbled mess? Probably the latter.

When designing your logo its best to use the old saying KISS, or keep it simple sweetie. Remember all those fine details still must make sense at any size. A rule of thumb is keep the words to the most important thing you need to get across. Anything else you need to say can be done visually with the design and images.

4.Not Thinking Black And White

Colors should most definitely be incorporated into your logo. We will go further into the logic behind color choice later, so I won't go into which colors to choose, but it is important you think about the variations your logo may be seen in. Your logo should be just as recognizable in black and white as it is in color. Take into account there won't always be a color copy option.

Think of Coca-Cola, or McDonalds. You would know the company even if there was no color to the logo. This means if your design is overly dependent on specific colors in order to stand out, you should reconsider changing it so it remains distinct with a clear message. If your logo design requires a fancy effect or a gradient to stand out- forget it.

5. Not Having A Message

As a startup consultant, I come across a lot of logos that say absolutely nothing. If you plan on investing money for marketing, please you everyone a huge favor and work to make your promotional material have a message.

Along your way of choosing a logo, you will want to find the ultimate symbol that will easily be able to grow with your company remaining relevant and on target. There are a few questions you should take a look at:

Who is my target market?

Who are my main competitors?

What differentiates me from my competitors?

What emotions/feelings do I want my logo to evoke?

What is my tagline and how can I make my logo work with it?

If you've already let your cousin make your logo, and now you are thinking of updating, think of the questions above. As you analyze how your current logo carries that messaging, think about what you don't like in your logo so that you can avoid making the same mistakes in the future. This analysis is important. Take your time and examine from all angles.

6. Picking Your favorite color

Green may be your favorite color but that doesn't mean it needs to be on your logo. Different colors have very different emotions that they emit. Later we will go into thorough detail about each color and the corresponding emotion it will cause your target market to feel. But for now, just know that it is highly likely your favorite color isn't doing your brand any favors.

Here is a quick list of do's and don'ts to keep you in line on your logo development.

Do use bold lines and simple shapes. Remember what I said about being able to be legible at a small size? This will ensure that.

Do make great use of negative space. This choice can take a boring average logo and make it look creative in 3 seconds flat. Take something away that can be implied and let your logo shine.

Do a few different logo options accessible at all times. You never know which one will be needed. At least one multicolor, monotone (one color), and a black-and-white version. I cannot stress to you how important these variations are. When you go to print your logo on shirts, embroidery, and coffee mugs etc., lots of "effects" may not be possible. The last thing you want is someone at the printing company altering your logo to fit specifications. You can't to be the one controlling how your logo is viewed.

Do ask your designer to also create a favicon of your logo for your website. (This is the little picture in the browser tab when you go to someone's site online, you want something there)

Don't use basic ornamental items like swipes and explosions. Unless you own a fireworks company, this serves no purpose whatsoever.

Don't and I repeat DO NOT buy your logo from one of those remade logo websites. I guarantee someone else will have your logo. It may not say the same words, but it will be the same style and concept. This may not bother you now, but when you become a national or international brand, you will have to replace it. Just skip this altogether and hire a graphic designer.

Don't forget about orientation. Let's say your logo is in landscape and you are having it included on a flyer with other logos of other companies, If the other logos are vertical or square, the designer may arrange them in a way that would cause your logo to be printed slightly smaller than everyone else's. If you have a logo designed in multiple orientations, you will be set to go when sending off your logo for work.

Don't go with anything trendy. As far as logo design tips go, this one is important: It'll be out of style before your target audience even sees it.

5 WHATS YOUR CATCHPHRASE?

We've got the visual representation on your company squared away with a memorable, efficient logo, now its time for the verbal representation- A tagline!

The tagline's role in branding is clear and simple: Tell your target market what your companies most important benefit, basically what sets you apart in a few compelling words.

It seems simple, but it is so much harder than it looks!

Think of a few tagline your sure to have heard, you can likely know who the company is even without the company name attached.

- A Diamond Is Forever
- Be All You Can Be
- Breakfast Of Champions

- Maybe She's Born With It

- Drivers Wanted

- MMMM MMM Good

- Once You Pop, You Can't Stop

All of these taglines have similarities that make them successful. Your brands tagline should also match the criteria in order to ensure people can not only relate and understand the messaging, but that they remember your tagline just as you remembered those above.

It is important that the tagline be unique to only you. It should be so different and tailored to your brand that it doesn't sound anything like any other tagline. You do not want to be mistaken for another company.

It should also be implemented in your business as much as your logo. You should use it consistently and liberally in order to really drive it home to your consumers. What good does a tagline do if it is only used on your business card.

Speaking of business cards, the tagline should definitely be used there. As a matter of fact any place that you have your logo positioned, if there is room, position your tagline as well. Think of them as a two for one package, where your logo is, there shall be your tagline. It tags along!

The most important characteristic your tagline should have

is the ability to be stuck in someone's head. It should be virtually unforgettable. You will always know "Just Do It" even if you have never bought a Nike product. Honestly, I have never understood the meaning behind "Just Do It" but it was brilliant marketing. The plastered that tagline everywhere. The even plastered it on the chest of millions of Americans. Let's be as memorable as that tagline.

Here are a few pieces to think about while creating your tagline.

Exercise 4

CREATE YOUR TAGLINE

1. Zero in on what makes your company different: write down the main benefit you provide that makes your company stand out above the rest.

_____
_____
_____
_____

2. Use that benefit to create a message that your target market will care about and understand.

_____
_____
_____
_____

3. Take that phrase and make it memorable. Use literary devices such as rhythm, rhyming, or alliteration to craft your phrase into one that's distinctive and easy to remember. Try putting a creative twist on a common phrase.

_____

_____

_____

_____

4. Is it short? Use as few words as possible, ideally five words or less. If you need to alter it, write the new version here.

_____

_____

_____

_____

Say it out loud. Speak the words to be sure the tagline is easy to say. If it's not, start the process over and keep trying. Keep at it until one rolls off of your tongue. Once it meets all the criteria, ask others what they think. Be sure to take other's thoughts into consideration but avoid the roundtable discussion.

Now that you have a tagline, implement it with your logo immediately. You are on your way to the world knowing what you stand for.

6 THOSE COLORS DON'T GO TOGETHER

Whatever color you choose for your business or for specific campaigns will have an impact on how people perceive your brand. I know I've said it a million times, but it is really important! Finally, we are at the section where we learn to choose colors.

I am in the business of fixing branding mistakes on a daily basis. I see way too many blatant horrendous mistakes when it comes to the use of color for business, however at times I am pleasantly surprised at the way companies get it right.

While there is not a "right" way to use colors, I can tell you right now, if you are doing it wrong there is one reason why: You don't know WHY colors (and color combinations) are important.

We all should know by now (I've said it numerous times at this point) Neuroscience and psychology proven time and time again that color can influence a consumers mood and buying decisions. It is influential a lot more than you may realize. Its why majority of places that sell food use the color red.

It's been shown that the color red can stimulate an appetite. This comes from our days as hunter- gatherers when we wanted to know if a piece of fruit or berries were ripe enough to eat without having to be close enough to smell it or touch it. For that reason, when we see read we think the food is good to eat, and then we are enticed to eat it. Pretty cool huh?

Blue and green are often seen as calming, more than likely because clear skies appear blue and fertile plains, and lush forests have a lot of green in them. These colors will make your consumers at ease and peaceful.

The really important meanings we derive from colors however, are dependent on cultural context. The significance of gold and green for "wealth" for example, come from gold's value as a precious metal, and because dollar bills have green in them.

Colors are not all received the same universally however. Far Eastern cultures for instance, associate white with funerals, while black fills a similar function in Western culture. Imagine using white in an ad for a hospital in a far east country thinking it would mean pure, but to them it signifies death.

As far as the United Stated goes, here is a quick guide to help with your choices:

- Blue: Trust, dependability, and strength.

- Red: Action and energy; can elicit a passionate response, but also aggression.

- Yellow: Optimism, positivity, motivation, warmth.

- Green: Nature and serenity. Can imply good health. Lighter greens = more peaceful. Deeper greens signify wealth or prestige.

- Purple: Creativity, mysterious, sophisticated.

- Orange: Energy, friendliness, confidence.

- Pink: Femininity, excitement, romance, and youthfulness. Light pink has sentimental tones, hot pink has high energy.

- Brown: Dependability, simplicity. Associated with nature, strength.

Those are just a few examples to get you started. The important thing is you choose a color that represents what your brand stands for. It's the consistency that forces the idea that certain colors and combinations "belong" to your brand. "What Can Brown Do For You?", "The Golden

Arches", "Big Blue" You already know who I am speaking of without me mentioning the company. The one and only reason we think to associate those colors with brands is because they have ingrained it in our minds through repetition. Once you have chosen colors to represent your brand be persistent and consistent.

You should also be thinking about what does and does not go together. This theory is based on the color wheel. Unfortunately, this book is in black and white, however any quick google search will point you in the direction of a color wheel. The following is how you know what colors go together and which do not. They are color scheme theories.

Complementary

Colors that are opposite from each other on the color wheel are said to be complementary colors (Like red and green) There is a high contrast of complementary colors that give a vibrant look. Complementary colors are tricky to use in large doses, but if you are looking to make a message stand out, this is what you need to go with. Complementary colors are really bad for text however, the contrast works against you in that situation so you should avoid it.

Analogous

Analogous color schemes use colors that are next to each other on the color wheel. Use them when you want to create serene and peaceful branding items. These colors while harmonious, can also be too similar. Be sure to have enough contrast in colors when choosing this type of color scheme.

Choose one color to dominate, a second to support.

Triad

This color scheme incorporates colors that are evenly distributed around the color wheel. Think of taking a floor from each corner if you were to place a triangle on top of the wheel. Triadic color harmonies are very vibrant, even if when using pale versions of the colors. To use this scheme the right way, use of the colors need to be carefully balanced. Let one color dominate and use the two others for accent.

Split-Complementary

Simply put, this color scheme is a variation of the complementary color scheme. Like the original, it uses a base color, but it also uses the two colors next to its complement. With this approach you get the same strong visual contrast as the complementary color scheme, but with less chance of it being a bit too much. For this reason, it is a great option for beginners.

Rectangle (tetradic)

This color scheme is made up of four colors broken into two complementary pairs. This is chosen for its ability to have many variations. It works best if you allow one color to be dominant and the others accent.

Square

The square color scheme is similar to the rectangle, but with all four colors spaced evenly around the color circle. The square color scheme also works best if you let one color be dominant.

Later when you chose your colors, pick a scheme that works best with your personal goals. Find a color wheel, chose a color based on the emotions you would like your target market to feel when they think of you, and apply one of the above-mentioned schemes to find your additional color.

Another likely problem is that you FAIL to develop and match your brand's colors for both print and web. This unfortunately is something I see on a daily basis when it comes to getting things printed for clients. Trying my best to make it simple, printing involves applying tiny amounts of dye (normally Cyan, Magenta, Yellow, and Black) side by side in small spaced, in the just the right proportions on a blank sheet so that your brain thinks its seeing any of hundreds of thousands of other colors. Your computer or TV screen reproduces color in a completely different way. It blends different-colored light (normally Red, Green, and Blue) in different proportions.

So super long, hard to understand, boring story short: You just can't make up colors on print and screen in exactly the same way (They use different colors) and this is why pictures on your computer hardly ever look just like they did on your screen, when you print them.

For this reason, it is always important to convert your colors from web colors to print colors. Ask your graphic designer for the actual code for the specific colors they use. It is not enough to say dark green, each color has a code for web as well as a code for print. Ask for it. If you have time to wait, ask for a proof of what you are printing before you are stuck with 1,000 copies of a flyer you though were red but arrived grayish pink.

Exercise 5

Pick Your Colors

1. Determine what you emotion you would like your target market to feel when seeing your brand. What color does that correlate with?

_____
_____
_____

2. Choose a color scheme approach

_____
_____
_____

3. Choose your primary palette colors

Okay, so now you know enough to begin choosing your primary or "dominant" colors for your palette. You'll likely only want two primary colors for this step. It's also important to note that one of these colors will be used a bit more than the other. Your dominant palette colors should either complement or contrast well together, and neither should outshine one another. Write your two-color choices (Which you have chosen by using the emotions list and the color scheme list) below.

_____
_____
_____

4.Choose your accent color(s)

Accent colors are just as important as the primary, don't let the word accent fool you. They work together to draw your consumers eyes to the thing you want to highlight. Without accent colors your messaging can appear flat, making it hard for the viewer to catch the point of your message.

Make sure your accent colors are bolder than your primary colors. Ensure that there's a high contrast between your primary and accent colors. Write your choices below.

_____
_____
_____

5.Apply your palette with the 60-30-10 rule

Now that you've finished choosing the identifying colors of your brand, its best you know the correct way to put them to use. There is no point in having a primary or accent color if you use them equally. The rule is as follows:

60% of your primary color,

30% of your secondary color and

10% of your accent color.

Think of a man in a business suit: 60% is the slacks and jacket, 30% is the shirt, and 10% is the tie."

By following the 60-30-10 rule, you will be able to use your colors in a way that is efficient and beneficial.

7 SOCIAL MEDIA, HERE WE GO

Social media is everything in this day and age. You need to learn it, use it and benefit from it. I often hear my clients say that it is too much to keep track of, or they don't know how to use it so they don't use it at all. If you are in that box, you are doing yourself a huge disservice. With social media you have the free power to reach your target market and influence their buying decisions as well as give them an introduction to you and your services.

Want to come out of the dark ages and going the rest of us? Want to know how to make social media work for you? Here's everything you need to know about using social media to build your brand:

1. Only choose networks that make sense for your brand.

There are hundreds of social media sites. There are about ten top social media sites that have a great pull on consumers. You don't have time to manage 10 sites and you're not at a place where you can spend the money to have one person do so, so don't.

Instead, find the platforms that support your brand image, taking the following factors into consideration:

Facebook is king! Three out of four adults in America have an active Facebook account. Facebook is a great platform for promoting pretty much anything because virtually any type of target audience can be found here. You most definitely need a Facebook Page.

If you are in the market to sell something that needs to be see, like food, clothing and other retail items, Instagram is your go-to. As the saying goes, a picture is worth a thousand words. It's also where the cool kids are. If your market is young adults, you'll likely find them here.

Google+ is great for reaching men in technology. Majority of their users are in engineering or some other tech industry. If this is your target market, you've found your haven.

Pinterest is the place to find reach women, stay at home moms and online buyers, especially for brands selling jewelry or clothing.

Finally, if you operate a business-to-business company, LinkedIn is the best choice for promoting business-related content and connecting with other corporate influencers.

2. Provide content that matters to someone other than you!

If you didn't know, your social media pages should focus on sharing snippets of information that your target market will find useful. Sure, you should post information on sales and what services you have, but honestly no one will follow you for that. However, if once a week you gave tips or something of value, you are likely to find yourself getting more and more subscribers.

Also keep these tactics in mind as you create content for sharing on social media:

Everything you create should match your brand. From the color to the tone, it would be consistent with your branding image. Humor is great but can be hard to execute well. If you know how to use memes the right way, they can be powerful brand-building tools. If you have no clue what a meme is, or are not sure how to incorporate humor, resist the temptation to create memes or engage in clickbait strategies. You may be setting yourself up to place your brand in a bad light.

Figure out which content will garner the most attention on your social networks. Do images resonate better with your audience than blog posts? You should be checking analytics weekly to check which your target prefers.

Use images! Images get more attention than posts without them. Even if you have no image to go with post, find an image that fits your brand and just use it as an accent. I promise you it will be much more efficient than posting without a visual.

One of the quickest and easiest ways to choose content for post on social media profiles is to study what types of posts your competitors have been successful with and put together your own, better versions.

If you see a competing brand has posted "12 Strategies for Closing the Sale."

Instead of wasting your time building content a based on a subject that's been untested, you could just create a similar but better post on the subject because you know there is an audience. For instance, you could put together a post titled "102 Strategies for Closing the Sale," or you could read your competitors version and from that create one that goes into more detail. Work smarter, not harder.

3. Use The Power of The Influencer

Great content is awesome! If you're new, you likely don't have that many people getting in oaths great content. It takes time to build an online presence. It's a slow and steady journey. A much faster approach is using someone in your industry who has already built this following. There are a few different ways you can do this:

Mention the names or cite the articles of the heavy hitters in your field.

Tag those you've referenced when posting to your social media profiles.

Email them to let them know you have referenced them in your content.

The goal is to get them to repost for you. Depending on the industry this can take a long time, or may be simplistic. It is important to attempt to build a relationship with these individuals. If all else fails you could go they pay route, however relationships always have more perks than money. You can't buy favor.

4. Run A Social Campaign

Organic reach for businesses on social media is all but dead. If you're looking to grow soles by someone finding you online, good luck. The sites have changed the algorithms on purpose to make it difficult for you to reach new people on your own.

To combat this, you may use strategies such as contests and other social media campaigns to successfully gain visibility and generate leads without having to purchase an ad campaign.

If you want to go this route, you will need to give your audience some valuable incentives that encourage them to participate. Be sure to make that incentive something everyone can find value in. Even though this is a powerful tool and one of the most powerful ways to reach new leads, it can be easy alienate people if you don't use it appropriately. That's what makes having a sound social media strategy set up so important. Key word being PLAN!

If you make it a priority to make a plan to approach social media, your brand building efforts are bound to pay off in the long-run.

Exercise 6

Let's make a plan

1. Create A Social Media Mission Statement

Your social media mission statement is going to be the beginning point for the rest of your decision making, so make sure you put some thought into it. This statement should make it clear exactly what you plan to use your social media presence. It should also align with the brand identity we worked so hard to create. Be sure to keep your target audience in mind.

_____

_____

_____

2. Identify How You Will Measure Success

How will you know if your efforts are successful? You need metrics, and I am not just talking about boosting your following. You are in business to make money, make sure your efforts are contributing to the bottom line.

A few metrics to consider measuring are:

- Conversion Rate

- Time Spent on Website

- Reach
- Brand Mentions
- Sentiment
- Total Shares

Most of the social media apps have a way to track all of these. Take advantage. Below write the ones that matter the most to you.

_____
_____
_____

3. Create and Curate Engaging Content

What will you be using to bring in the crowd? Here are a few suggestions.

- Images
- Videos
- Blog Posts
- Company News
- Infographics
- eBooks
- Interviews

I strongly recommend that you create a content calendar

that outlines how often you will post to each network, which topics you will share and when you will share them. Write your choices below.

_____
_____
_____

4. Invest in a Social Media Management Tool and Make a Schedule.

There are numerous apps that will allow you to pre-schedule your content to be released. You only have to do all the work once, and after that you can be absent minded for a while. Below write down the schedule you would like to stick with when posting.

_____
_____
_____

Each previous step should be reconfigured after you have some time to let it run its course and analyze the results of your marketing efforts. Let the data drive you. Whatever you see if having the best results, stick with. What is not working well, ditch it.

8 DON'T CHEAT YOURSELF, TREAT YOURSELF

Ok, so we have taken the time, created great brand guidelines and now you're going to start implementing them throughout your company. But two months from now, you need to design new flyer for aa new initiative you're launching, and you think it would be great if you can pick a color or two outside your color scheme, even though you know better.

Why undo all the hard work we've done and make it hard for your target market to remember you by changing everything up. There is so much out there that brands and messaging get lost even when staying consistent. Its hard for your audience to keep up. They need help to remember your brand. The second you are inconsistent, then someone else will show up and steal their attention away from you.

It's important you are offering your customers with a consistent experience in every aspect they encounter. No matter if its viewing your website, or your social media pages, online advertising, even television commercials, or even an ad in the local paper, the branding and messaging should remain the same.

As you've learned, it is the face of your business. People grow to trust your "brand", change the face and they may no longer recognize it. That trust then goes out the window. They won't know how to tell the difference between your super awesome business, and the basic one that popped up on their Facebook feed.

To bring it home and nail it in, it is a no-no to start changing the color of your logo to match with a background color, or distort it by stretching it to fit inside an image frame. Messing with the consistency of your brand can break the relationship of trust you have worked so hard to build with your clients. So, for the sake of your business growth, stay consistent!

And with this I leave you a better, more educated business owner. I know you will used the skills taught to place into the world a great brand that will be successful and presented in the best light. Let no one deter you from your guidelines and Good Luck!

ABOUT THE AUTHOR

Myi Baker is a top expert on small business branding. She is an idea oven, brand problem solver, and creative powerhouse working at the intersection of branding, marketing and social media. As the founder of Houston, Tx based branding firm Myind, Myi has helped countless businesses create consistent, efficient and memorable brands well as leverage mainstream media and blogs and social media campaigns to build buzz online and off.